# QUICK GUIDE TO CUSTOMER SERVICE

PRESENTED BY GIANCARLO HERNANDEZ VELA

I dedicate this book to my family, and especially to my wife, Rommy Valer. This book would not have been possible without her love, support, and patience. Thank you for always being by my side, even in difficult times. Your unconditional love and trust in me have given me the strength to keep going and pursue my dreams.

# CONTENT

# INTRODUCTION

Customer service is one of the most important parts of any business, as it is the way in which a company interacts with its customers before, during, and after the purchase of a product or acquisition of a service. Good customer service can not only enhance the customer experience, but also increase customer loyalty, the company's reputation, and ultimately, its financial success.

Customer service has become even more crucial due to modern trends in consumption. Customers have more choices and access to online information, which allows them to compare prices, products, and services quickly and easily. Social media and other digital platforms have given customers a platform not only to learn about companies but also to express their opinions about them and their experiences. This means that companies must be more proactive in their approach to customer service to ensure a positive experience and avoid reputational harm.

One of the most significant trends regarding customer care is personalization. Customers expect companies to understand their individual needs and preferences and offer customized solutions to meet them. This can be a challenge, especially for companies that handle large volumes of customers. However, companies that strive to provide a personalized experience are more likely to retain their customers, increase their loyalty, and attract new prospects.

Another important trend in customer service is automation. Companies are increasingly using technology to provide more efficient and faster customer service. For example, chatbots and virtual assistants can answer common questions and resolve issues without the need for human intervention. Automation can improve customer service efficiency, but it can also result in an impersonal and frustrating experience for customers if not done correctly.

Customer service is also critical during times of crisis. Companies must be prepared to handle unforeseen situations such as service disruption due to system failure, natural disasters, public health issues, or supply chain disruptions that may affect the customer experience. In these moments, a company's ability to provide alternative solutions and exceptional service can make the difference in its survival, long-term success, and differentiation from the competition.

Empathy and speed in customer service are also fundamental. Customers expect companies to care about them and their individual needs. Offering personalized solutions, acting quickly on their problems creating a sense of urgency, and even apologizing for mistakes are current expectations in every customer. Companies that can demonstrate empathy are more likely to retain their customers and maintain a positive reputation.

Transparency is also important as customers expect companies to be honest and transparent in their communications and policies. Lack of transparency can create mistrust, directly and negatively affecting the customer experience.

In summary, customer service is a critical aspect of any business. In an increasingly competitive and digital environment, the quality of customer service has become even more important for customer loyalty and satisfaction, as well as for the reputation and financial success of the company. In times of crisis, a company's ability to provide exceptional customer service can make the difference in its survival and long-term success. Therefore, it is essential that companies focus on providing high-quality customer service, both in normal times and in moments of uncertainty.

# UNDERSTANDING CUSTOMER NEEDS

Understanding customer needs is a fundamental part of any business strategy, as it allows for the provision of products and services that are relevant and valuable to a user, whether they are direct customers of a company or not.

Knowing these needs opens up a world of possibilities for the company, from implementing or correcting measures in the customer service process to adapting or launching products, all with the aim of capturing users' attention. And not only that, but having this knowledge allows for the implementation of innovative solutions and personalized attention to their concerns and problems.

In addition, understanding customer needs is important in order to provide exceptional and differentiated service, which can help to retain customers, increase their loyalty to the company, and reduce the risk of migrating to the competition. This may include quickly resolving issues and being able to adapt to changes and customer expectations.

Likewise, knowing customers and their needs allows for a focus on creating a competitive advantage focused on constant innovation and adaptation to market trends, as well as the implementation of effective marketing strategies that allow for effective customer outreach.

And it's that the evolution of marketing and the understanding of the customer and their needs have gone hand in hand for a long time. Thus, we can identify three very distinct stages.:

1. First stage, which was focused on generating the product or service itself, without knowledge of the consumer or their needs. These products and services aim to satisfy needs from the company's perspective and the advertising used was traditional, such as radio, television, or print media. This stage is also known as Marketing 1.0.

2. The second stage focuses on the consumer and their intrinsic needs, and then seeks to satisfy them with the products and services that can be generated. Companies focus on getting to know their consumers and not just on achieving numbers for sales; they seek to create emotional value that attracts and retains their customers by

providing value in interactions in the pre-sale and post-sale stages. This stage is also known as Marketing 2.0.

3. The third stage focuses on seeking the deeper needs of the customer and building a deeper relationship with them. Companies already know that satisfying needs is not just about launching products to the market, so through this Marketing 3.0, companies, among other factors, focus on satisfying the emotional and collective needs of customers (and letting them know) while also building customer loyalty.

To identify and understand customer needs, it's important to establish effective communication and a trusting relationship. This can include conducting interviews or surveys with the customer, or direct observation of their purchases and consumption patterns.

It's essential to listen carefully to what the customer has to say and ask questions to clarify any doubts or ambiguities.

Listening attentively to the customer and asking questions to clarify any doubts is a fundamental part of identifying and understanding their needs. By paying attention to what they're telling us, we can gain valuable insights into what they require now, what they crave in the short and long term, their consumption expectations and preferences, among others.

Furthermore, by listening and asking questions, it demonstrates to the customer that they are valued and that there is an interest in understanding their needs. This can help establish a relationship of trust and foster customer loyalty to the company.

It's also important to keep in mind that attending to the customer's voice can help avoid misunderstandings and resolve problems in the short term and more effectively. For example, if the customer has a complaint or problem, it's essential to listen carefully and ask specific questions to understand the situation and provide an appropriate solution.

Just like in the continuous improvement process, the work cycle is cyclical, continuously seeking to "improve" from the starting point, the customer listening process has the same structure that begins with listening to the user and ends with listening to the user:

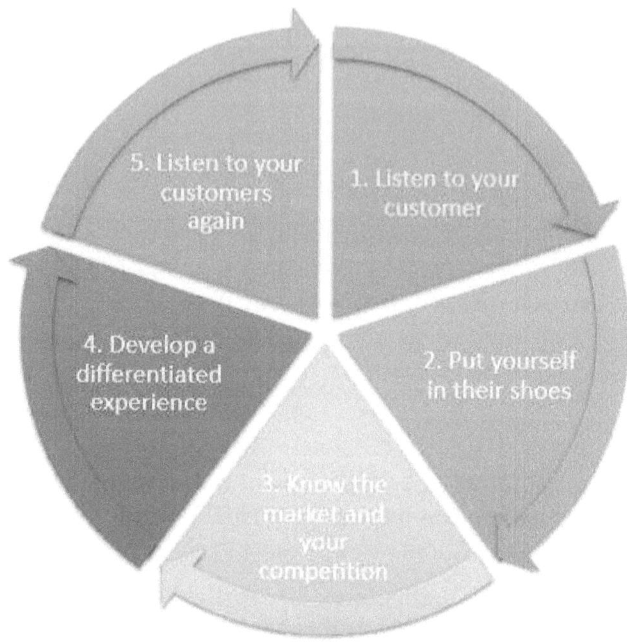


Just as in the continuous improvement process, the work cycle is cyclical, constantly seeking to "improve" from the starting point, the process of listening to the customer has the same structure, beginning with listening to the user and ending with listening to the user.

In any relationship between two or more people, understanding the way of thinking is not enough to understand behavior. Empathy is needed, that is, seeing reality from the customer's point of view for a better understanding of the situation and reactions.

Customers generally react mainly under two basic concepts: they will seek to satisfy their needs under the best conditions and will feel loyalty to the provider who provides the best experience along with the best benefits. Needs can be met in various ways, but providing a differentiated and unique experience while meeting a need makes the customer want to repeat the same experience over and over again.

Another way to understand customer needs is to analyze the market, direct competition, and products that could be considered substitutes. This can help identify trends in the market, unmet needs, and partially met needs, as well as determine how to offer a unique and differentiated product or service with high value for the customer.

In addition to identifying and understanding customer needs, it is also important to provide appropriate and effective solutions to meet those needs, with services that involve the customer in an innovative experience. This can include customizing products or services to adapt to the specific needs of the customer, or implementing customer service measures to address any problems or concerns.

It is also necessary to keep in mind that customer needs may change over time, so we must be alert to these changes and adapt to them in a timely and efficient manner. To the extent that companies can adopt this adaptability to changing customer and market trends in their culture, they can provide new products and services or adapt existing ones to these trends more quickly than their competition, obtaining a competitive advantage in the market and the attention of customers who will see their expectations met more efficiently.

In the past, car users only looked for the benefit of personal transportation or moving their goods from one place to another. Later, the implementation of certain levels of safety and comfort inside the vehicle was added as a benefit. Today, with technological advances in the automotive industry, customers are seeking other benefits. For example, driving assistance systems, 360-degree cameras, parking sensors, touchscreens, and online connectivity are just some of the features that have been added to make vehicles more attractive to customers.

Another example of how a product can be innovatively modified to meet customer needs is through customization. Companies like Nike allow customers to customize their sports shoes to fit their specific tastes and needs, such as choosing colors, materials, and designs. This allows customers to get a product that fits their needs and preferences exactly, providing them with a more personalized and satisfying shopping experience.

Finally, another way to understand our customers' needs is through feedback and input, where valuable information can be obtained on how well their needs are being met and what aspects can be improved. This can include collecting customer comments and opinions through surveys, interviews, or social media, or observing customer behavior patterns to identify areas of opportunity. It is important to use this information effectively and make the necessary adjustments to improve the customer experience and maintain their long-term satisfaction and loyalty.

As an example of this, let's imagine that a manager of a women's clothing and accessories store receives comments from several customers through the company's website, saying that they love the quality of the clothing, but that they find it difficult to find their size in some products. In addition, some customers suggest that they would like to see more variety in styles and colors.

In this case, customer feedback has provided valuable information about their needs and desires. You can use this information to make improvements to your business and better satisfy your customers' needs, such as expanding inventory with more sizes based on customer demand and the stock of best-selling sizes in recent months, expanding the range of styles and colors, and offering discounts to customers who take the time to provide feedback in order to encourage continued customer participation and demonstrate that their opinion is valued.

# ESTABLISHING SERVICE EXPECTATIONS

Establishing service expectations is an important part of service quality management in any company or organization. It involves defining and clearly communicating what is expected of the service provided to customers or users, both in terms of quality level and availability and accessibility.

In other words, service expectations comprise all the actions and responses established as a service procedure, all the services provided, and the predefined quality standards delivered to the customer. Since each of these responses and quality level is specific to the company's service, customers assume and demand that they are always met, becoming the minimum expected from the company.

To establish appropriate service expectations, it is important to consider the needs and expectations of customers and users. This involves conducting market research and competitive analysis; tools such as surveys, interviews, or focus groups with customers to understand their needs and expectations can provide valuable insights for decision-making.

Once service expectations have been identified, it is important to establish specific goals and objectives to meet these expectations. These objectives should be measurable and achievable and should include timelines for their achievement.

It is also important to establish an action plan to ensure the fulfillment of these service expectations. This plan should include a series of concrete steps to ensure that the service is provided effectively and efficiently and should include both preventive and corrective measures. In this regard, here are some steps you can follow to establish this action plan:

1. Identify your customers' expectations.
2. Evaluate the service you currently provide to your customers.
3. Establish clear, achievable, and measurable goals to improve your current service.
4. Establish specific actions and responsibilities that involve the entire team to achieve the set goals.

5. Set up a customer service team training plan based on the findings of the current service. These trainings should be sequential and continuous with an evaluation at the end of each one.

6. Conduct progress tracking and evaluation to establish progress and necessary adjustments to achieve the set goals.

Communication with customers is key to establishing and maintaining service expectations in optimal conditions. It is important to inform customers and users about how the service is provided and how problems or suggestions can be reported. The active communication channels for addressing the needs and questions of customers and users should always be clear to avoid unmet expectations.

For example, if a company has implemented a chat on its website to communicate with customers who have inquiries and requirements, but after some time it decides to open a customer service channel on WhatsApp (considering it easier to use and more personal with users), replacing the chat, they should communicate to customers what the current communication channels will be and from what date the chat on the website will be deactivated. This is to avoid some customers unnecessarily searching for the chat option and not finding it, thinking that the company does not have the contact channels enabled.

Staff training is another key aspect to ensuring compliance with service expectations. It is important to ensure that staff is always well-trained in the necessary processes and procedures to provide quality service. It is also important to provide employees with the tools and resources necessary to perform their job efficiently and effectively.

At this point, it is recommended to avoid high turnover rates among customer service team members, as the learning curve is generally high, and it is common to see how the service indicators of such a channel are affected.

Time management is another necessary aspect to ensure the fulfillment of service expectations. It is important to establish appropriate deadlines and schedules for completing tasks and attending to customers, and to ensure that these times are consistently met.

The problem with not defining times for different tasks is that there may be idle time during work hours, or more minutes or hours may be allocated to manage a task with lower demand, or conversely, a very limited time may be set for tasks that require a longer management time to maintain quality.

As we can see, setting service expectations is an important part of customer service management, as it allows our customers to know what to expect from the service we provide, and employees to have a clear guide on what to provide in each interaction or task.

It is also important to establish clear and achievable goals and objectives for customer service. This may include reducing waiting times, improving problem resolution, increasing service levels, or achieving a certain level of customer satisfaction. These goals should be measured and reviewed regularly to ensure the fulfillment of service expectations and identify areas for improvement.

Another crucial point is training and development of staff to perform their job duties and any additional tasks that may be required due to workload demands. Employees should be equipped with the necessary skills and techniques to provide exceptional service (not just regular or mediocre) to customers. This training should include the use of tools they will use in their daily management. Additionally, they should be informed about the service expectations, how their position contributes to meeting those expectations, and what actions they should take.

Furthermore, it is important to establish appropriate communication channels for customers to provide feedback, ask questions, provide comments, or submit complaints. This may include setting up a customer service hotline, a contact page on the website, implementing various types of surveys, or providing the option to send emails or direct messages through social media.

If non-direct contact channels such as mailboxes, surveys, or social media communication are implemented, it is important to have a trained team to attend/analyze such communications and to have an immediate response text informing the receipt of the message, thanking for the communication and time spent, so that the customer feels that the company pays attention to their needs and opinions.

It is essential to ensure that all company employees are committed to customer service and understand the importance of meeting service expectations. The fulfillment or non-fulfillment of such expectations could directly affect the image and even the reputation of the company if dissatisfaction is not timely addressed and corrected.

Finally, I believe it is always necessary to communicate a company's service conditions to customers to be transparent and not create impossible expectations. This communication should be clear and precise, for example, by publishing service policies within service agencies or creating a brochure that clearly describes service quality standards and the processes that must be followed to serve customers. As a friend always says, "Clear communication from the beginning always clears up any doubts".

# EFFECTIVE COMMUNICATION WITH THE CUSTOMER

Effective communication with the customer is essential for conveying ideas and transferring knowledge to another person or groups of people. It involves the transmission and reception of messages through various means such as writing, speech, gestures, images, videos, or expressions.

However, in some cases, this attempt to convey ideas may not achieve its purpose because the message is not clear enough, the channels used are not the most suitable, or the context in which the message was sent was not ideal for conveying the message.

On the other hand, effective communication goes a step further, where the message is conveyed in an understandable and clear manner without any doubts on the part of the recipient. In other words, when effective communication is achieved, the central message, its meaning, and its intention are understood.

In the business world, communication should always be effective so that messages emitted by the Marketing and Customer Service areas are transmitted correctly, as well as the central ideas of the products that the company provides, their benefits compared to the competition, and how they solve a customer's problem or concern.

Effective communication can improve customer satisfaction, foster customer loyalty, and increase sales. One key element is always starting with active listening to the customers. This means paying close attention to what our customers say, asking questions to clarify their message, and showing interest in their needs and concerns.

Once we understand what the customer is saying, it is important to respond clearly, accurately, and with complete information, providing relevant and useful information according to the customer's message.

In addition to actively listening and responding to customer inquiries, it is important to be kind and empathetic with each customer. This can help calm anger, decrease worry, and can help establish a relationship of greater trust.

Empathy helps to better understand the needs and concerns of the message sender and to provide a more personalized and satisfying service. To achieve this, we must ask various questions to better understand the perspective and feelings of the customer, which will show the customer that we are interested in them and their needs. Often sharing personal or third-party stories related to the same topic that the customer is discussing can help humanize the relationship and demonstrate that we care about the people behind the transactions, not just about providing services or products.

Transparency is also an important component of effective communication with customers. It's important to be honest and open with customers about any issues, delays, or observations that may arise. Providing a sincere explanation and, above all, an action plan to resolve the issue can help reassure the customer and show that their concern is being taken seriously.

I want to emphasize that service companies must be one step ahead in solving their customers' problems. If one of our users has an unforeseen issue with their request, which will be delayed or observed, the customer service department must contact that customer informing them of the real status and possible solutions already evaluated so that the customer can make the decision about which one to choose. However, only informing the problem (without the solution) or waiting for the customer to define the path to take should never be done.

The above implies having good internal communication between the company's departments in order to provide a comprehensive diagnosis and possible solutions, seeking consistent and high-quality service despite the inconvenience. Therefore, it's necessary to have clear protocols and flows, where each team knows its functions according to the type of scenario that arises, always accompanied by a plan for continuous training for employees, ensuring that all team members are aware of the company's policies and procedures, as well as current regulations.

Effective communication also involves knowing when and how to use different communication channels. For example, some customers will always prefer face-to-face interaction with an executive, others prefer to speak on the phone, while others want to communicate via email or through social media, and finally, there are those who prefer to self-serve through an application or the company's website. Therefore, it's important to be available through various channels to meet our customers' different communication needs, despite the market trend towards digital channels.

In an interconnected and technological world, it is unthinkable not to use the tools that technology puts at our fingertips. Therefore, I mention 5 options that can improve communication with customers that apply to any business:

1. Implementing the classic mass email system: You can use email marketing tools to send personalized emails to your customers with special offers, product or service updates, and other relevant information. I recommend using certified domains to ensure that your emails do not get blocked or diverted to the spam folder

2. Developing an online chat: It provides a fast and effective way to communicate with your customers and respond to their questions or concerns in real-time. Nowadays, it is possible to include a bot in this alternative that solves the most frequent questions that customers have. For this, you should identify the 5 or 6 most consulted topics (the main ones) and transfer them as options within the bot so that the customer can self-serve and only request the attention of an executive in case they cannot resolve their query.

   Now, if you want your bot to be one step beyond ordinary, you could configure it to allow identity validations according to security protocols and provide access to restricted information from your clients' accounts. For example, once the security filters are passed, the customer could obtain a code that arrives by SMS (with a certain validity period) so that, by entering it into the bot, they can access certain certificates, reports or account statements.

3. Creating an online community: Establish an online forum or group for your customers where they can share their experiences, give suggestions, and provide feedback. A good idea for this is a customized blog where you can expose success stories, resolved problems, experiences of star clients, product news, sector-related news, etc.

4. Using social media: Social media platforms like Facebook, Twitter, Instagram, TikTok, and LinkedIn are an excellent way to reach your customers and maintain active communication with them. Beforehand, you should perform an analysis of the target market you want to reach and the content you will create since the audience that uses LinkedIn is very different from the one that uses TikTok.

   In the 21st century, a company that is not on social media is literally dead.

5. Organizing events and webinars: Offer your customers the opportunity to participate in in-person or online events where they can learn about your products or services, try them out (if possible), and ask questions directly to your team. These events can also be an excellent way to encourage interaction and build lasting relationships with your customers, creating differentiation from other companies in the market (not only direct competition).

# KPI AND MEASURING CUSTOMER EXPERIENCE

The key performance indicators, commonly known as KPIs, are important as they allow you to have results that show whether a product or service is efficient, satisfactory, or within the required minimum standards.

For the case of Customer Service, KPIs will allow us to measure and evaluate whether the company's contact with its customers through its service channels is efficient and of quality. These metrics and their results will provide a systematic, evolutionary, and real analysis of how the team of service channels and support teams perform their functions and how the customer experience is affected by them.

While measurement is important as it reflects performance, the most important thing is the tracking and analysis of each result in order to find elements that need adjustments or improvements in order to improve customer satisfaction and experience.

Many companies focus only on one or two indicators related to customer service (in some cases more), but their results do not fit into the company's strategy, so they are not given the appropriate weight to make high-impact adjustments. By this I mean that if the company does not internalize that the relationship with its customers is the main thing within its operations, constantly measuring to find deficiencies or improvement points, it will not be able to retain and retain its consumers, but rather runs the risk of having a constant flow of customer migration to the competition.

Having indicators in Customer Service allows for understanding the performance of the department and each customer service representative, identifying breakpoints and bottlenecks, reducing response times, making better business decisions, creating strategies that impact customers, creating loyalty and recommendation with third parties.

Based on my experience, I can point out that there are many types of KPIs, which can be modified and adapted to the needs of each company (according to the reality it faces), but I would recommend considering the following:

1. Service Level. This indicator basically measures whether the teams of different customer service channels are equipped to meet the demand for

customer service under a predetermined standard.

Achieving a high percentage in the service level implies that the company has the capacity to meet the market demand or the current situation, while a low level will demonstrate that the number of professionals should be strengthened, the assigned machinery increased, or the technological equipment strengthened, depending on the analysis conducted.

If your company is dedicated to the manufacturing or distribution of certain equipment or appliances and your service level is low, you should consider increasing your inventory to fulfill orders and deadlines. For this, you will need to evaluate acquiring or improving your machinery (in case you are a manufacturer) or purchasing larger volumes if you acquire the product from third parties.

On the other hand, if your company is dedicated to customer service by phone calls and you identify that you do not cover the demand for incoming calls, you should consider increasing the number of positions after evaluating whether the increase is due to temporary or consistent reasons. This evaluation will allow you to decide whether such positions are temporary or permanent.

2. Response time. It is the time it takes to attend to a request, requirement, or procedure from the moment the customer presents it.

   In customer service, this indicator will vary depending on the type of channel through which contact is established with the customer. For example, for an in-person service agency, this time covers from the moment the customer enters the office until the service is completed. For a call center, it covers from the beginning of the connection until the call ends. For messaging systems such as WhatsApp or Messenger, it covers from the first message sent by the customer to the last one responded to by the service representative.

   For this measurement, many companies that work with call center teams and messaging systems only consider the interaction with a representative, but not the time used in the interaction with the bot within the system (almost all these services have a bot configured to provide specific information and segment the service), which is a mistake because from the customer's perspective, the time used to contact the company starts from when the call enters or the first message is received.

   Here are some statistical data to consider: more than 45% of customers expect their inquiries to be answered in less than 4 hours, and 12% expect a response within the first 15 minutes. Customers who contact through messaging systems such as chat or WhatsApp expect a response within the first 35 seconds.

3. Number of complaints and claims received. This indicator allows understanding which area, product or service has the most problems within the company.

   It is important to remember that a complaint and a claim are a customer's expression of dissatisfaction with a product or service offered by a company and directly affect customer satisfaction and recommendation. The expression of this dissatisfaction should be received through virtual or physical means available to the customer, where the company can obtain the greatest details of such dissatisfaction (details that will be valued when giving a response and identifying improvement points).

   Complaints are more focused on the perception of the service offered while claims focus more on the tangible. For example, in a restaurant, a complaint could focus on dissatisfaction with the delay in service or because they did not take the complete order, while the claim would focus on the delivery of a dish with spoiled meat or the utensils delivered to use during dinner being dirty.

   Each complaint and claim must be considered individually and responded to in the same way. It should be considered that what applies to one case will not necessarily fit another, therefore the response must always be personalized.

It is important to note that ideally, no complaints or claims should be received, but that is not always the case. Statistics and controls of complaints and claims received can be carried out daily, weekly, monthly, quarterly, semesterly, and yearly, making comparisons of the evolution of the claims received and responded in favor of the customer or the company.

We will further expand on the topic of complaints and how to deal with them in a later chapter.

4. Complaint and claim resolution time. This is a complement to the previous indicator and allows measuring the average time it takes to issue a response to a claim or complaint.

   Both the previous indicator and this one are typically standardized by an entity that supervises complaints and claims filed by users. The aim is to respond to these types of expressions quickly and to ensure that the content of the response is focused on the central issue expressed by the customer.

   The measurement of this indicator should consider the analysis time of the person or team assigned, as well as whether there is any referral to another area to obtain crucial information to issue the response.

It is recommended to create a system (for example, in an Excel sheet, a dashboard, or an external system) that allows identifying when the time assigned to gather information or formulate the response is taking longer than the assigned time, and there is a risk of failing to meet the response time. This system could use a traffic light approach to flag delays.

5. Customer Satisfaction Level (CSAT). This measurement seeks to quantify the level of satisfaction of customers on a scale based on their interactions with the company. The evaluation is carried out through a survey using a basic and direct question such as "How satisfied are you with the company?" or "Are you satisfied with the company?"

   This satisfaction or dissatisfaction can arise from the purchase of a product or the delivery of a service, but above all, how the customer has perceived it.

   This indicator allows obtaining detailed and descriptive data of a recent interaction where it will be manifested whether the company met the customer's expectations or not.

   The CSAT survey regularly uses a scale of 1 to 5 under the Likert scale:

   - Very dissatisfied
   - Dissatisfied

- Neither satisfied nor dissatisfied
- Satisfied
- Very satisfied

To obtain the satisfaction index, it is only necessary to calculate the percentage of positive ratings (numbers 4 and 5) out of the total number of responses.

After obtaining the indicator, it is necessary to analyze the positive results to identify best practices, and the negative results to propose improvement or change actions.

6. Net Promoter Score (NPS). This measurement seeks to quantify the level of customer recommendation within a scale that ranges from 0 to 10. The evaluation is carried out through a survey using a question: "How likely are you to recommend our product/service/brand to a family member or friend?"

   Customers who respond with a score between 9 and 10 are considered promoters of the company and are expected to speak positively about the company. Customers who rate with a 7 or 8 are considered neutral, and although they may be satisfied with the company, they are not convinced to recommend it. Finally, customers who rated between 0 and 6 are considered detractors, and their opinion is that the company is bad and would not recommend it.

The NPS is calculated by subtracting the percentage of detractors from the percentage of promoters, which results in a number ranging from -100 to +100.

A positive NPS can be considered good, while a negative NPS indicates that there are problems that need to be addressed. Although this evaluation is not always applicable since each company's standards and objectives are variable.

In my opinion, the evaluation of the NPS goes beyond the CSAT since a user may be satisfied with the service delivered by the company but would not recommend it to a close person since they are not entirely convinced. Recommendation is a step ahead of satisfaction since it seeks others to experience the good experience that has been lived.

Finally, I must point out that the measurement of the NPS can be carried out under the relationship or transaction approach, that is, the recommendation of the company is based on the overall experience with the company or focuses solely on the last interaction that has been had. Many companies use the transactional NPS as a base and constant indicator, while the relational one is executed once or twice a year.

7. Conversion rate. The conversion rate seeks to provide a statistic focused on the probability that a customer will buy a product again or upgrade a purchased service. It can also be understood as the ratio between the number of users who visited the website or an agency and the number of users who purchased a product or service after that visit.

   For example, if 25,000 people accessed your website in May and 1,000 made a purchase, the conversion result would be dividing 1,000 by 25,000, generating a value of 0.04, which in percentage would be 4%.

   This indicator is extremely important as it allows identifying if the efforts made in the location, marketing, advertising, personnel, and service and/or product are transformed into income for the company.

   If the indicator is low, it means that adjustments must be made by evaluating the most critical and costly processes versus the simplest and fastest modifications.

8. Retention and churn rate. The customer retention rate seeks to identify the percentage of customers who, having entered the company in a short period of time, have not moved to the competition but continue to acquire products and/or services from the company.

On the other hand, the customer churn rate can be understood as the number of customers who stop using the products and/or services of a company to use those offered by the competition. These customers are not willing to make a new purchase or stay in our company.

As we can see, customer churn equals current and future economic losses for the company.

For example, if for each month of a year, 100 customers purchased your products worth $100, your company would make a profit of 100x12x100 = $120,000. But if your churn rate is 20% for the following year, the income will be as follows: 80x12x100 = $96,000. In other words, churn cost the business $27,000.

Most companies invest a lot of money in attracting new customers, but few focus on ensuring that customers continue to make purchases. So, for any business to increase its profits and sustain over time, it is very important to have a low churn rate and a high customer satisfaction rate.

# PROBLEM RESOLUTION AND COMPLAINT MANAGEMENT

A complaint is a formal or informal expression of dissatisfaction or discontent about something, whether it's a product, service, or situation. For example, a customer may make a complaint about the quality of a product or the treatment received from an employee.

A claim, on the other hand, is a formal demand or request for a solution or compensation for a problem or dissatisfaction. For example, a customer may make a formal claim to a company to obtain a refund or a solution to a problem with a product or service.

The key differences between a complaint and a claim are formality and intention. Complaints can be informal and a solution or compensation is not always expected, while claims are more formal and seek a concrete solution to a problem. In addition, complaints can be a simple expression of dissatisfaction while claims seek an action from the company for a solution.

However, receiving a claim should not be considered a negative point for the company, but rather as feedback from customers to improve the service and product. The problem arises when there is no strategy to analyze the claims, no plan to mitigate future increases in these, and no protocols for providing a comprehensive solution in the shortest possible time.

Now, receiving a claim can be a challenge, but there are certain steps and attitudes that can help to go through these moments without unleashing a storm and, if possible, helping the customer in the midst of their discomfort:

1. Listen carefully: Listen carefully to what the customer is saying and make sure you fully understand their problem. Give them the opportunity to express their feelings and concerns without interruptions, taking note of every detail of what the customer expresses.

2. Keep calm and courteous: This is basic. Maintain calm and courteous behavior at all times, even if the customer is upset or angry. Remember that it is important to maintain a professional and respectful attitude to resolve the situation, especially if the reason for the complaint is due to the company itself.

3. Take notes: I mentioned this in point 1. Take detailed notes of everything the customer is saying to ensure you don't miss anything important and to have accurate documentation of the complaint or claim. The timing, details, and every situation are important to build the entire framework of the claim.

4. Offer solutions: Once you have understood the problem, the central point, and every detail of the discomfort, offer concrete, realistic, and perceivable solutions for the customer. Work with the customer to find a solution that satisfies their needs and expectations, but be the one to propose the alternatives. Never wait for the customer to take the initiative for the solution as they will understand that the company does not take the initiative to provide a viable path.

5. Follow-up: This can be interpreted in two ways: one making the complaint or claim your own, and the other seeing the post-response changes from the complaint. A) Once you have received the complaint, and as far as possible, follow up on the case until it is resolved, consulting with the areas that will intervene in each stage of the resolution process, ensuring that the time to take action is not exceeded, and finally informing the customer about the solution provided by the company. B) After resolving the complaint or claim, follow up to ensure that the customer is satisfied with the solution, considering making changes to your processes or policies to prevent similar problems in the future.

6. Remember that the goal is to effectively and satisfactorily resolve the complaint or claim for the customer, which may require patience, empathy from the customer service representative, and collaboration from the operational areas to resolve the claim and improve to avoid similar issues in the future.

As mentioned earlier in this chapter, it is important that resolving a complaint is considered a critical activity for the company, where the competent areas responsible for providing part or all of the response consider this activity as the most critical at that time. Strategy is everything.

Therefore, I present some ideas on how to incentivize a service culture in operational areas, but mainly, the perception of criticality when responding to a customer complaint:

- A company's vision where customer service is one of the central pillars, and it is shared with the staff, will enable every collaborator to be aligned with the path the company considers as the one to follow. The vision should always be communicated clearly and periodically reminded to ensure its due importance.

- Operational teams should be trained not only in the technical and practical aspects of the company's products and services but also in how to effectively interact with customers. Training employees in soft skills, such as empathy and active listening, is essential to foster a customer service culture.

- It is important to recognize and reward collaborators who excel in resolving complaints and meeting their goals. A performance-based incentive system can motivate employees to strive for achieving their objectives, improve customer satisfaction, and problem resolution.

- The company must establish clear processes for resolving complaints, from the reception of the complaint to its final resolution. Creating a complaints and claims handling procedure is fundamental to achieving goals, but it is an uncommon practice in small and medium-sized companies. Employees must be aware of, internalize, and follow these processes to ensure a quick and effective resolution.

- Providing constant feedback to employees regarding their performance in terms of customer service and problem resolution is the second step to achieve the next level, as creating goals and rewards is necessary to measure performance. This feedback should be constructive and aimed at improving, never focusing on highlighting mistakes and unmet goals.

- Fostering a culture of continuous learning is essential to creating a culture of service and criticality. Employees should feel comfortable sharing their experiences and learning from each other in an open environment, not limited to comments or experiences that favor the company or management.

In summary, instilling a culture of customer service and criticality in a company's operational teams requires a comprehensive approach that includes a shared vision, ongoing training, results-based incentives, clear processes and procedures, constant constructive feedback, and a culture of learning, all within a framework of transparency to express oneself freely.

Finally, it's important to know that not all people who work in customer service activities are trained to handle complaints and critical customers. These activities require a higher level of certain qualities that must be developed over the years. I detail some of them below:

- Empathy: Ability to put oneself in the customer's shoes and understand their needs and expectations.
- Patience: A critical customer can be demanding and difficult to please, so being able to remain calm in tense situations is essential.
- Active listening: Every customer service representative must be a good listener and have the ability to identify the customer's needs.

- Effective communication: Delivering clear, accurate, and concise information is of utmost importance when providing a response to a complaint or claim.

- Problem-solving skills: We should not be stuck on the problem, paralyzed by the situation. We must be able to identify and resolve customer problems effectively.

- Product and service knowledge: Individuals who handle a claim must have a deep understanding of the products or services offered by the company, beyond surface-level features, to offer effective solutions to customers.

# TIME MANAGEMENT

Time management is valuable to individuals because time is the one thing that cannot be recovered once it's gone. People have a limited number of days in their life, and the time they have available is precious to achieve their personal and professional goals, to enjoy life, and to spend time with friends and family.

Time is valuable to businesses because time is a limited and non-renewable resource. Companies have a limited amount of time to achieve their objectives and goals, and if they don't use that time effectively, they can lose opportunities, revenue, and customers.

Effective time management for individuals can improve the quality of life, reduce stress, and increase the sense of personal achievement. For businesses, it can improve productivity, reduce stress, and increase profitability.

Here are some definitions of what time management is from various authors:

"The management of time is the ability to take control of the amount of time you dedicate to everyday activities, in order to achieve your goals and objectives" (Tracy, 2001).

"Time management is the process of planning and exercising control over the time spent on activities, with the purpose of increasing effectiveness and productivity" (Covey, 1989).

"Time management is the practice of planning and controlling the time spent on different tasks and activities, in order to achieve greater productivity and efficiency" (Drucker, 2005).

In other words, time management is a key skill for anyone who wants to be productive and achieve their goals in life. It is a skill that can be learned and improved through practice and the implementation of effective techniques.

Time management focuses on maximizing the time available for tasks, minimizing stress and anxiety, and achieving a healthy balance between work and personal life.

Time management is a key aspect in the business world. Companies and businesses have specific deadlines and objectives that must be met to be successful. Therefore, it is important for business leaders to understand how to manage their time and how to teach their employees to do the same. Time management can help companies be more efficient, save time and money, and improve overall productivity.

One of the keys to time management in the business world is proper planning. Business leaders should plan their workday and set priorities for the tasks and projects that need to be completed. Planning helps reduce the likelihood of distractions and allows important tasks to be completed without interruptions.

From personal experience, I must say that when I was young, I started my workdays with my mind always on the pending tasks from the previous day and progressed as I remembered and the current day's tasks were given to me. I learned that keeping a list of tasks where I can assign priority or criticality to those tasks allowed me to better attend to daily activities without neglecting those tasks that are of high priority.

One of the most popular techniques for time management is the Eisenhower matrix, which divides tasks into four categories: important and urgent, important but not urgent, not important but urgent, and not important and not urgent. This helps prioritize tasks and focus on what is truly important.

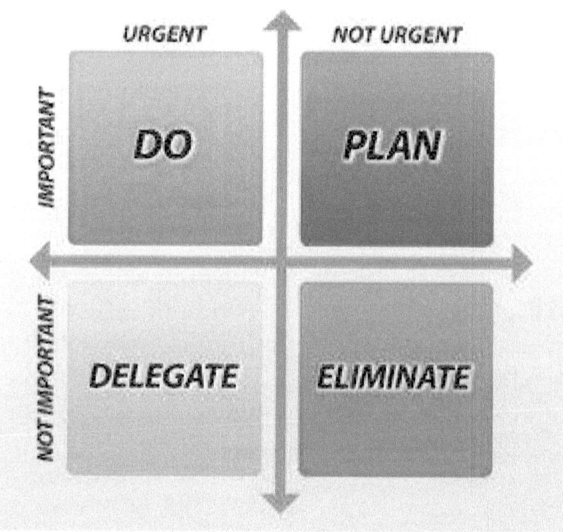


The Pomodoro technique is another time management technique that involves dividing work into time intervals, usually 25 minutes long, called "pomodoros," followed by short breaks of 5 minutes. The technique is named after the use of a kitchen timer in the shape of a tomato (in Italian, pomodoro) that was used to measure the time intervals.

Here are the steps to implement the Pomodoro technique:

1. Choose a task that you need to accomplish.
2. Set a timer for a 25-minute pomodoro.
3. Work on the chosen task for the duration of the pomodoro.
4. Once the timer rings, stop working and take a 5-minute break.
5. After completing four pomodoros, take a longer break of 15-30 minutes.
6. Return to step one and repeat until the task is completed

The idea is that by breaking your work into time blocks and taking a brief break after each block, you can maintain your focus and productivity while avoiding mental fatigue and burnout. You can also use the technique to adjust your work and rest time according to your needs, which will help you be more efficient and reach your goals.

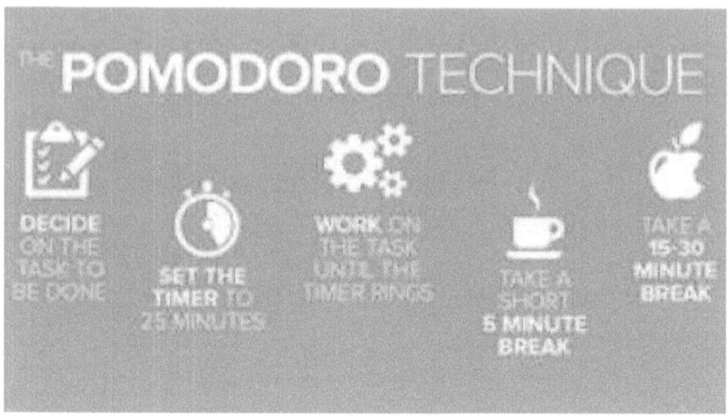


Another useful technique is the use of time management tools, such as calendar apps or task management apps, which allow scheduling activities by importance, setting reminders, assigning deadlines, among other features. In addition, these tools allow synchronization across different devices and collaboration in teams, making it easier to coordinate and organize work.

The use of technological tools can be of great help in time management. Time management and productivity apps allow for planning tasks, scheduling reminders, setting goals, and monitoring progress, among other functionalities. This can improve efficiency and help reduce time spent on less important tasks.

Time management also involves setting clear and achievable goals. Goal setting helps prioritize tasks and work with purpose. In addition, it is important to celebrate achieved milestones to maintain motivation and continue moving towards long-term goals. (Díaz, 2021).

Another time management strategy is task delegation. Delegation not only involves sharing responsibilities with others, but also trusting their ability to perform certain tasks. This way, time can be freed up to focus on other important tasks, which can improve efficiency and reduce stress. (Fitch, 2019).

Another important but often overlooked aspect of time management is the elimination of distracting elements. Leaders must ensure that their work environment and that of their team is free from distractions such as external emails, text messages, phone calls, and unnecessary meetings.

Social media and online browsing can also be a major distraction in the workplace, although I believe that interconnectedness is part of the world we live in. Many of the applications used in businesses are online (unless a purchased license is available), so limiting online consumption can limit productivity to some extent.

But in conclusion, time management is essential for business success. By implementing effective time management methods and eliminating or reducing the number of distractions, concentration can be improved and efficiency in daily tasks can be increased, whether at home or in business.

# TEAMWORK AND COLLABORATION

Teamwork refers to the collaboration of two or more individuals to achieve a common goal. It is an effective way to achieve results that could not be accomplished if each person worked individually.

It is a collaborative strategy in which several people come together and strive in an organized way to achieve a common goal. In the business context, teamwork can improve efficiency, productivity, and the quality of results. It helps to foster creativity, innovation, and diversity of thought in a business environment.

There are two definitions about teamwork:

"Teamwork is a collaborative process between two or more individuals with complementary skills and knowledge, who come together to achieve a common goal through interdependence, effective communication, coordination, and shared commitment" (Hackman, 2002).

"Teamwork refers to the interaction and collaboration of a group of individuals to achieve a common goal through shared commitment, mutual accountability, and coordination of individual efforts" (Katzenbach & Smith, 1993).

As we can see, the concept of teamwork is related to collaboration, commitment, interdependence, coordination, and communication. While independent tasks are important and have their own significance, tasks that involve the involvement of multiple people working together in a coordinated way to achieve the same end, attain a milestone, or fulfill an objective, require a different level of complementarity.

For different people, sometimes from different areas, to work together to achieve a goal, it is important to follow certain parameters, establish teamwork practices, and define individual tasks. Below are some recommendations for achieving effective teamwork:

1. It is of utmost importance that each team member can communicate clearly with the other members. This requires effective communication channels, a clear code or language, and real-time communication tools.

2. Each member must understand their role, the functions they must fulfill, and their responsibility within the workflow or project. Each supervisor or manager should monitor and ensure that each participant carries out the assigned activities.

3. All team members must have a clear understanding of the project's objectives and goals. Goals should be specific, measurable, achievable, relevant, and time-bound.

4. It is important to establish a clear process for decision-making within the team. Different options should be discussed, and a consensus reached on the best decision, as well as the empowerment to have authority and freedom to act in the best way for the client or project.

5. Conflicts may arise within the team, and this may be more common than expected, but it is important to establish a process for conflict resolution that allows team members to resolve their differences constructively without affecting the client or the company.

Now let's look at some examples of how teamwork can be applied to various situations:

1. It is common for a company to form a team with people from different areas in order to design, develop, and ensure the success of a new product, service, or improvement to an existing product. Each team member brings their own unique perspective, skills, and experiences to contribute to the project.

2. When a problem or crisis arises within a company that affects the normal course of activities, it is beneficial to form a high-performance team to analyze and provide a range of solutions and measures to mitigate the risk of similar situations in the future.

   By working together, the team should examine the problem from different angles based on their profiles and experience in order to reach the best solution.

3. When a company needs to carry out a large-scale project such as implementing a new software system, expanding into new markets, or opening a new plant/branch in a new region or country, it can form a dedicated team solely for that project.

   The team will work to ensure that the project meets the established regulatory and regulatory requirements, is completed within the set timeline using the allocated budget, and above all, meets the company's objectives.

4. In a restaurant, when a customer approaches the counter to make a special request in their order, which would deviate from what was previously established on the menu, if all team members work together and communicate effectively, they can ensure that the customer's request is properly addressed. The waiter will quickly relay the customer's request to the chef, who in turn will inform his kitchen staff to be attentive to the customer's order. Time and quality of the order are of the utmost importance, so working together and in a coordinated manner will allow the customer to receive their order exactly as requested, which will improve their overall experience and increase the likelihood that they not only return to the restaurant but also recommend it to others.

5. In a retail store, if a customer approaches with a complaint that they were given a defective product, if team members work together, are flexible, and give high priority to the complaint, they can address the customer's complaint efficiently and satisfactorily. For example, a team representative can speak with the customer to better understand the reason for their complaint, while another member verifies the defective characteristics of the product based on the customer's opinion. With the analysis done, alternative solutions should be sought to resolve the problem, such as correcting the defective

characteristics (if possible) or providing a new product in replacement of the defective one. If the entire team collaborates and works together effectively, they can quickly and efficiently resolve the customer's problem, which will salvage the customer's experience.

In summary, teamwork can significantly improve the customer experience by ensuring effective and efficient communication, as well as a quick and satisfactory solution to any problems that arise.

# CUSTOMER SERVICE THROUGH MULTICHANNEL: SOCIAL MEDIA, WHATSAPP AND ARTIFICIAL INTELLIGENCE (IA)

The customer service has evolved over time and has experienced significant changes in the way it is provided.

The basic and traditional way of attending to customers was in-person, where customers would visit a physical store to receive or purchase a product or service they deemed necessary. Later on, with the progressive advancement of technology, it was implemented that customer service could be done or complemented with a phone call to ask questions, receive help, request information about certain products, purchase a product or service, and even to file a complaint.

However, with the arrival of technology and the popularity of the internet, customer service has evolved and it is now possible to provide assistance to customers remotely and virtually.

The development of customer service has been driven by various technologies, including email, chat applications, and social media. These tools allow customers to contact companies online and receive answers to their questions, purchase a product or request a service within minutes. Moreover, the availability of information online has allowed customers to solve problems on their own without having to contact a customer service representative, that is, through self-service systems.

This remote assistance has allowed companies to offer support to customers without the need for physical contact, as remote assistance includes telephone assistance, online chat or email, or other electronic communication media. This multi-channel approach allows customers to have various options for assistance where their inquiries, requirements, and complaints can be received and attended to from any point on the planet. This means that for the customer, it is easier to contact the company from anywhere, and for the company, it can increase the number of contacts with its customers.

In addition, virtual customer service has allowed for greater efficiency in service. Companies are looking to automate their processes, move their services to remote or virtual channels, and where possible, use artificial intelligence to provide immediate assistance to customers. Chatbots, for example, can answer common questions and solve simple problems without the intervention of a human representative. However, when configured correctly, they can also implement customer authentication (simple or complex) to deliver confidential information or reports that were previously only available in-person.

Along with these multiple improvements, it is also necessary for customer service representatives to acquire knowledge of the technologies the company implements and the services that are transferred to new channels. This way, their service is no longer the only available channel, as it once was, but rather complements the attention of an intelligent service that was previously configured.

From the company's point of view, the number of customers served is increased, and the cost of maintaining physical equipment, agencies, and representatives in agency modules is simplified.

The development of channels like WhatsApp and social media has had a significant impact on how companies provide customer service. These communication channels are highly popular among consumers and offer an easy and fast way to interact with companies.

In particular, the use of WhatsApp to provide customer service has become increasingly popular. Customers can send messages directly to companies through the app and receive real-time responses. This provides a convenient way for customers to make inquiries or resolve issues without having to wait in long queues or wait for email responses.

Social media has also had a significant impact on customer service. Companies can use platforms like Twitter and Facebook to interact with customers, answer their questions online, and promote their services and products.

However, the use of channels such as WhatsApp and social media also presents challenges, especially those related to response speed and security. These channels may be considered highly informal for business services by consumers, and many customers may expect a quick response, which may not necessarily arrive. For example, placing a pizza order through Messenger or WhatsApp can be a challenge if the consumer is in a hurry and the company has few service executives, although it can be streamlined if a bot is implemented within these tools to provide customer service based on frequent responses.

As we have already mentioned, modern companies must be able to handle multiple queries at the same time or establish service flows where customers can self-serve without the intervention of a customer service representative whose limit of simultaneous attention is limited.

I provide two examples of how the implementation of a remote and virtual customer service channel can improve the customer service experience and level of service:

- During the Covid-19 health emergency, many companies were forced to suspend their activities due to mandatory social distancing and quarantine measures imposed by different countries. Only those that could implement or already had remote service systems in place were able to maintain contact and services with their customers. Virtual chats, email support, WhatsApp, and Messenger were tools that allowed customers to request products and services or inquire about the status of their requests, as well as enabled companies to maintain the necessary cash flow to keep the business afloat during such difficult times.

  Many customers who had active contact channels with companies that provide services or products during this phase of their lives concluded that their experience was very satisfactory, and their loyalty grew, as they saw that their needs were not ignored, but that there was an effort to address them in times of crisis.

- While channels such as WhatsApp or Messenger provide alternative means of addressing customer queries without the need to travel to a specific location, such as an agency, they do not necessarily allow for the completion of critical processes and requirements or the retrieval of confidential information quickly and securely. In these cases, a good alternative is to transfer a customer identity authentication system to a secure site on the company's website, so that critical processes (if possible, those with the highest flow) can be carried out through this secure site, such as updating critical data (personal or banking data), or placing or disposing of money using bank accounts (automatic debit or withdrawal of available balance).

  An insurance company carried out the activities described above by evaluating which processes are most required by its customers and which are viable for implementation on its website. The results were surprising, as not only did customers use these processes recurrently, but there was also a migration in the flow of attention for these processes from physical channels (previously, 80% of interactions were in-person at an agency) to this new virtual channel (after implementation, 90% of customers were served through the website), reversing the balance of results.

While new technologies have transformed the way companies interact with their customers, allowing for faster, more efficient, and personalized attention, it does not mean that they are eternal or immovable. There are new discoveries and developments that companies are gradually starting to implement and use within their protocols and attention flows that improve the customer experience and service level. Among them we can mention:

- Artificial Intelligence: Artificial intelligence (AI) allows companies to analyze large amounts of data to better understand the needs and preferences of customers. AI can also be used to personalize the customer experience, provide recommendations, and improve efficiency in customer service.

  AI is also being used to analyze customer opinions and emotions through data mining and natural language processing. This helps companies better understand the needs and preferences of their customers, and personalize their services and products accordingly.

  AI allows companies to collect and analyze large amounts of customer data, enabling them to personalize the customer experience based on their preferences and behaviors. This can include product recommendations, offer personalization, and delivery of personalized marketing messages.

- Automation: Business process automation or robotic process automation (RPA) allows companies to automate routine tasks such as data entry, inventory management, and order tracking.

This can reduce response times and improve efficiency in customer service.

Here is a shortlist of some of the most popular RPA tools for modern businesses: UiPath (has an intuitive and user-friendly interface, allows for text and image recognition), Automation Anywhere (offers a wide variety of solutions for process automation, has machine learning tools to automate complex processes and improve efficiency), Blue Prism (focuses on critical business process automation such as invoice processing and inventory management), and Pega (focuses on end-to-end process automation up to customer experience optimization).

- Collaboration Platforms: Collaboration platforms such as Slack and Microsoft Teams allow customer service teams to work together more efficiently. These tools allow for information sharing, task assignment, and real-time collaboration, which can improve problem-solving and customer satisfaction.

In summary, the development of channels such as WhatsApp and social media has had a great impact on customer service. These channels have provided an easy and fast way for customers to interact with companies, significantly improving the customer experience. However, they also present challenges that companies seeking to offer effective customer service through these channels must address.

# CUSTOMER SERVICE IN CRISIS SITUATIONS AND BUSINESS CONTINUITY

A crisis situation for an organization refers to a situation in which the company faces a significant threat to its ability to operate and/or remain profitable. This can be caused by a variety of factors, such as a decrease in demand for its products or services, an interruption in its supply chain, a natural disaster, a legal or regulatory issue, poor internal management, a reputation crisis, among others.

A crisis can have a negative impact on the company in terms of its public image, profitability, ability to retain employees, and ability to meet the demands of its customers. In addition, a crisis can affect other stakeholders, such as suppliers, customers, shareholders, and the community at large.

Companies should be prepared to reduce the likelihood of entering crisis situations, deal with them, which involves having a risk identification and contingency plan in place, and having the ability to make quick and effective decisions to minimize damage and recover as quickly as possible. Therefore, it is necessary for every company to work on a business continuity plan alongside risk identification.

Regarding customer service, a crisis situation refers to an unexpected event or circumstance that negatively affects the flow of attention and customer experience of a company or brand, and that can have a significant impact on their satisfaction, loyalty, and perception of the brand.

These situations can include errors in the delivery of products or services, technical issues, delays in response to inquiries or complaints, and more serious situations such as natural disasters, supply chain interruptions, or public scandals.

Below are some definitions of crisis situations related to customer service:

- "A customer service crisis situation occurs when customer expectations are not met due to a problem with the service, which can lead to dissatisfaction that may affect the company's image" (García-Martínez, Pérez-Martínez, & Moliner-Tena, 2019, p. 60).

- "A customer service crisis situation is an unexpected event that has a negative impact on the relationship between the company and the customer, and that may put the company's reputation and financial stability at risk" (Cruz-Ferreira & Biedma-Ferrer, 2020, p. 128).

- "A customer service crisis situation is a critical moment in the relationship between the company and the customer, in which the way the situation is handled can be decisive for the success or failure of the company in terms of customer loyalty and satisfaction" (Valencia & Sandoval, 2018, p. 47).

We can mention several risk situations, some of which may include:

- Failure of the main database servers, which prevents regular service as there is no access to customer account information.

- Failure of one or more service providers' servers that affect the virtual channels implemented for customer service.

- Cyber attack that compromises the security of accounts and information stored by the company.

- Security breach due to impersonation and theft of information.

- Natural disaster events such as an earthquake, landslide or tsunami.
- Fires in agencies, buildings, or nearby facilities that endanger the safety of staff or customers.
- Health emergency that prevents in-person customer service.

Now, creating a risk plan for business continuity is an important and necessary task to ensure that the organization can continue to operate in the event of unforeseen crises and interruptions. Below, I present you with some steps to create a risk plan for business continuity:

1. Identify the risks: The first thing to do is to identify the risks that could affect the business. These risks can be natural (such as earthquakes, floods, storms), technological (such as IT system failures), human (such as strikes, intentional disasters), or anything else that could interrupt operations.

2. Evaluate the impact of each risk: Once you have identified all the risks, it is important to evaluate the impact and criticality that each identified risk would have on your business if it were to occur and the likelihood of this happening. This will help determine which risks are more critical and

which may be more frequent, but above all, will allow efforts to be prioritized in mitigation planning.

3. Develop mitigation strategies: After evaluating the impact, criticality, and possible frequency of each risk, you must develop strategies to mitigate them. It will be necessary to implement contingency plans for each risk scenario, periodically backup critical customer and company data, create alternate attention flows in case main channels fail or stop working, create alternate methods or channels to maintain customer service levels, among others.

4. Establish a work plan and crisis response team: It is important to establish the step-by-step approach of how to face a crisis scenario (by type and criticality) when it is happening and a response team that can make quick and effective decisions. The response plan must be approved by each management and shared with all areas of the company for the knowledge of all employees. Likewise, the team must be composed of qualified members from different areas of the business and must be trained in how to respond to different scenarios.

5. Test, review, and update the plan: Once the plan has been developed, it is important to test it to

ensure that it works correctly. The test should include different risk scenarios and ensure that all stakeholders understand their role in the crisis response. In case modifications or adjustments are needed because the practice does not match what is indicated in the plan or because there was a change in operations or technologies used, proposals for modification should be communicated to the areas involved and updated according to the findings. However, to ensure that the plan remains relevant and effective, testing and reviews must be periodic.

When it comes to customer service, the negative expectation from a total or partial system failure can be quite a challenge, but there are some practices that can help manage the situation. Here are some tips:

- The first thing to do is to acknowledge that there is a problem and accept responsibility as a company. It is important for every customer service representative to be honest and transparent about what has happened and the actions being taken to resolve it as soon as possible, as misinformation or failure to provide information (which are different) can be powerful tools for speculation and dissatisfying even the most demanding customers.

- It is important to put yourself in the customer's shoes and understand how each one feels, that is, to be empathetic with the customer. The system failure or complete or partial paralysis of business activities may have caused inconvenience, delays in deadlines, failure to submit files, delay in processing a previously submitted application, or loss of money. Understanding each concern and showing empathy can help build or restore trust and at the same time reassure the customer.

- Offering a solution or action plan can help regain the customer's trust as we are providing an alternative to the problem. At this point, proactivity and ingenuity are crucial to rescue the service. This could include tracking the incident until it is resolved to inform customers waiting for a solution (I recommend always using personal channels such as phone calls or WhatsApp messages), fixing the problem (if it is within the representative or area manager's functions), offering a refund or compensation for the inconvenience caused (if it is company policy), among many other actions. For example, if the system has crashed and we have a customer waiting at our agency, we can take note of their contact information and the requirement they seek to make so that when the system flow is restored, a designated team can call them and guide them to make their request remotely/virtually or provide them with the information they were looking for.

- Learn from the experience. Once the problem has been resolved and the crisis state has been lifted, it is important to analyze what has happened, the activities carried out in the midst of the crisis, as well as the customers' reactions and look for ways to avoid them happening again. With this, the customer service protocols and manuals should be updated, if necessary, as well as the work plan for a crisis.

A while back, a Peruvian friend worked for a pensions and insurance company that was always characterized by innovation. They were always looking to improve their processes, products, and customer-facing services to benefit their clients, which sometimes led to modifications of existing regulations.

When the state of emergency was declared due to the COVID-19 health crisis, all their nationwide branches had to close and in-person services were suspended overnight in March 2020. In response to this, they had to activate what they called their "Virtual Agency", which had been in the testing phase, receiving only certain requests and providing very limited service.

The challenge was to transfer 100% of the procedures and requests that could be carried out in a physical agency to the new virtual agency while maintaining the same warmth, speed, and efficiency that had characterized them before. Therefore, the company took three clear steps as quickly as possible:

1. Converted all the paper-based requests into virtual format to be used for future remote assistance.

2. Enabled remote work for all agency personnel by dividing them into two teams to handle requests and requirements related to clients' or employers' accounts, as well as pension and withdrawal processes.

3. Promoted the new remote assistance channel through its Virtual Agency, highlighting that the assistance has not stopped and its clients can count on the professionalism and closeness of their company.

The decision-making, organization, and implementation of the plan only took 3 weeks, so by early April 2020, the service had been restored. This generated great expectations from customers, allowing for a significant increase in satisfaction levels and recommendations compared to the competition, who had not reacted promptly to the crisis or projected themselves to develop remote customer service.

# CONCLUSIONS

In conclusion, customer service is a critical aspect for any business that wants to succeed in today's market. In a world where customer needs and expectations are constantly evolving, it is essential that companies understand and adapt to customer expectations in order to provide a satisfying and memorable experience.

Measuring the customer experience is key to determining whether or not customer expectations and needs are being met. Companies should use metrics such as customer satisfaction (CSAT) or Net Promoter Score (NPS) to get a clear idea of how customers feel about their experience with the company. These metrics can be used to identify areas for improvement and take action to improve the customer experience.

In addition, in today's digital age, it is essential for companies to modernize their customer service strategies and use new technologies to provide better customer service. Technologies such as artificial intelligence, machine learning, and chatbots can help companies provide faster, more efficient, and personalized service to customers. Social media is also a powerful tool for companies as it can be used to directly interact with customers and address their questions and concerns.

In summary, customer service should be a priority for all companies. Companies that focus on understanding customer needs and expectations, measure the customer experience, and use new technologies to improve customer service will have a competitive advantage in today's market. At the end of the day, it all comes down to providing an exceptional customer experience and building lasting relationships based on trust and satisfaction.

# REFERENCES

Covey, S. R. (1989). The Seven Habits of Highly Effective People. Paidós.

Drucker, P. F. (2005). The effective executive: The definitive guide to getting the right things done. HarperCollins.

Tracy, B. (2001). Eat that frog!: 21 great ways to stop procrastinating and get more done in less time. Berrett-Koehler Publishers.

Díaz, C. (2021). Importance of establishing goals in time management. Retrieved from https://www.iberdrola.com/talento/establecer-metas

Hackman, J. R. (2002). Leading teams: Setting the stage for great performances. Harvard Business Press.

Katzenbach, J. R., & Smith, D. K. (1993). The discipline of teams. Harvard Business Review, 71(2), 111-120.

Cruz-Ferreira, E., & Biedma-Ferrer, J. M. (2020Social media as a customer service tool in crisis situations. Journal of Business Studies, 2(1), 127-143.

García-Martínez, M., Pérez-Martínez, P. J., & Moliner-Tena, M. Á. (2019). Effect of customer service on customer satisfaction and repurchase intention. Journal of Marketing Research, 21(1), 57-72.

Valencia, R., & Sandoval, E. (2018). Managing customer service in crisis situations: a literature review. Journal of Administrative and Social Sciences, 5(1), 41-54.

www.ingramcontent.com/pod-product-compliance
Ingram Content Group UK Ltd.
Pitfield, Milton Keynes, MK11 3LW, UK
UKHW040030200726
13854UKWH00001B/451

9 798215 170205